# MEMORIES OF
# OLD FIFE

Carol McNeill

First published 2015

ISBN 978-0-9934753-0-6

Published by
Fife Publicity
fifepublicity@btinternet.com
www.carolmcneill.co.uk

Printed by
Multiprint (Scotland) Limited, Kirkcaldy
Telephone 01592 204755
www.multiprint.tv

Acknowledgements:

Very many thanks to all those people who told me about their lives and work over
the years with such kindness and patience. It was a great privilege to listen and to
share their memories. They include Mrs Adamson, Mrs Allan, David Balfour,
Bella Barker, Ken Bowman, Nancy Brodie, Harry Briggs, Tom Carrington,
Wullie Colville, John Crichton, George Currie, Effie Ewing, Dr Senga Greig,
Ina Hutchison, Mrs Lambert, Janet Meikle, Hugo Melville, Kate Miller, Annie Napier,
Margaret Ness, Minnie Paris, Anne Penman, Bob Ritchie, Abe Simpson, Jim Swan,
and many others who preferred to remain anonymous.

Front cover image courtesy of St Andrews Preservation Trust

# Chapter One
# DAILY LIVING

"It was like a but and ben, a kitchen where you cooked, ate and did everything really and the bedroom was next door. There was no water indoors, just a tap in the yard and an outside toilet. There was a space under the back door which was handy in the summer because you kept the milk bottles there to keep them cold, but in the winter you had to stuff old coats underneath to keep out the draughts. The women spent a whole day washing the family's clothes by hand after they lit the boiler in the outside wash house."

Families in the early and middle years of the twentieth century had a very different way of life than that of today. Household items which are now thought of as necessities were either luxuries or simply not available at all. Housing in Fife, as in other parts of Scotland, was often basic in the extreme, often with outside sanitation, and it was usual for two or three generations of the same family to live in one house with extended family members next door.

There were few if any of today's modern conveniences. "I was born in 1909 and we had paraffin lamps which were filled up every morning," said a Fife woman. "Most of the houses round about paid for their own gas going in because it didn't look as if the landlord was going to do it. Every house had a kitchen range, ours was very modern to our eyes and you did the cooking on it. Some of the older ones had an oven, a tank for the water, and the fire in the middle. My mother had the old kind of iron where you heated up a bolt on top of the range and put that in the iron to heat it up. I used to hate when she told me to do some ironing, so if I was needing out to see my pals I would rattle the bolt until my dad would say, 'Oh get finished and go away out to play!'"

A Kirkcaldy man recalled his childhood from a distance of more than eighty years. "My grandfather had a big hut in Johnnys Loan, he let the poachers keep their nets in it and he got a rabbit as a reward. He was a good cook and he made some braw rabbit stew for us. My other grandfather was a kiln man at Morrison and Crawford's pottery - there was a pub over the wall and the men would put pails over and pull them up filled with beer."

The basic living conditions were tempered by the strong sense of community which has been diluted over time. "Poverty made us all good friends. There maybe wasn't much in the cupboard but everything was kept as clean as soap and water could make it. The curtains were snowy white and the doorsteps and sills had patterns with pipeclay. No-one locked doors at night, we were all friendly and we had nothing worth stealing anyway."

It was usually people in professional or business classes who owned their own homes, with rental the more usual course of action. One determined woman however found a way to achieve her own home. "My grandmother always wanted to have her own home, but this was in the 1890s and she had no money really," said

The old houses in Oswald Road were built in the late 1890s, with outside wash houses and toilets which would have been shared by several families.

Linen manufacturer Robert Philp left a trust fund to build four schools including this one in the Links area of Kirkcaldy.

a Thornton woman. "There was all this ground on the Station Road, and a lawyer advised the families to form ourselves into a group and he would make a draw: someone would get the first house, someone the second - it was like the beginning of a building society. My grandmother walked to the lawyer's office in Kirkcaldy with her baby in her arms, and put the little girl's hand in and drew out the first ticket. So they got the first cottage and paid so much per month which would have been very difficult indeed, but it was the one thing in her life she wanted."

Schooling was often elementary at the start of the twentieth century, when money was tight and there was nothing left for school clothes or books. Kirkcaldy youngsters were luckier than most, thanks to linen manufacturer Robert Philp who founded a Trust Fund which provided two schools in Kirkcaldy, one in Linktown (then a separate burgh) and one in Kinghorn, all managed by a board of governors. The scholars received grants for clothes as well as a sum of money when they left school. When Philp died in 1828, almost his whole estate of £70,000 went to the Trust, a huge sum in those days. His headstone in Kirkcaldy's Old Kirk graveyard must be unique in that his earthly assets are inscribed on it in detail. He was not the only businessman to be concerned about the education of the next generations; in Dunfermline, Erskine Beveridge, another linen manufacturer, built St Leonard's School in 1860 for the children of his workers as well as establishing a works library.

Half-time schooling was still in existence in the early 1900s, when pupils attended school in the morning and went off to work in the afternoon. It was probably seen as a compromise between getting a basic education while bringing in some much-needed money for the family. "I went to half-time school, I think that finished before WWI," said Kirkcaldy man Abe Simpson who was born in 1903. "Money was tight, but I had a very kindly aunt who gave me a couple of shillings which was an awful amount of money then." His determination to get a good education stood him well, as he joined the Fire Service and finished his career as Deputy Firemaster for Fife in 1965.

And a Pittenweem man took a pragmatic view of his school days. "I wasn't very clever but I enjoyed it, and I left school at 14 though you could leave at 12, but you learn more after you leave school. When you served your apprenticeship you took more interest and made the effort to learn."

Punishment for bad behaviour at school was the dreaded strap, belt or Lochgelly tawse. "My father said when he was a wee boy, his teacher was awful handy with the strap," recalled a Thornton woman. "When he came out of the class one day he lifted the strap from her desk, shoved it up his jersey and ran for home. The men were building the new school at the time and they could see he was upset, so he told them what had happened. The builder was working on the walls and took the strap, put it on top of one of the stones and put cement on it, and said "You'll never get the strap with that one again, it's built into the school!"

A farmer's daughter who attended a country school said that she walked to school at 8 am each morning. "We took a piece with us because there were no school meals. There were two classes for the three Rs and in the afternoon the girls had sewing and boys got woodwork. I left school at 12 because we needed the money."

Thornton School was built in 1904; perhaps a wee boy's strap is still hidden in the walls?

The Norwegian ship *AW Singleton* was dashed on the rocks below Wemyss Castle in the great storm of October 1898.

Before the electronic age, children played with what was around them, chalking out 'pauldies' on the pavements and playing shops using broken pottery for coins. Girls had skipping and ball games, knitted long strips of wool on a peg with four nails, or collected paper scraps and swapped them with friends. "My favourites were the angels sitting on clouds, and the best ones were 'pre-wars' - which would have been pre-WWI as they were Victorian ones on thick paper." Boys had cigarette cards, put pennies on tram lines to see them get flattened, ran for miles with their iron girds, rolled down the empty streets inside an old tyre and then as now, played football.

One woman commented on how easily children now get bored. "Being bored didn't come into it when we were young, if you wanted to go to the beach then maybe four mothers would get together with the children and all took pieces to eat and played on the sands. There were no public libraries but the Co-op gave you a catalogue and you ticked off the books you wanted from them, we always had plenty to do."

Children were largely unaware of what was going on in the wider world, but one tragedy in particular did strike home. "I can remember the *Titanic*, the shock of 1500 lives lost, it was a terrible thing," said Abe Simpson. "It was supposed to be unsinkable, and it was a tremendous shock to the public that a ship like that could sink, they hadn't thought about the icebergs." And Wullie Colville, born in 1906, recalled: "I remember seeing the paper boy on the corner with a big paper bill pinned round his waist with the dreadful news: '*Titanic* lost with most hands,' it was April 1912."

Many older people now remember the freedom of their childhood with nostalgia. "The prettiest part of the Fife coast to me was between Wemyss Castle and the Glass Cove," said a Coaltown of Wemyss man. "We had a great time during the summer holidays - racing, climbing trees, hunting for crabs and building rafts. I remember when a Norwegian barque was driven ashore during a gale, and got firmly wedged on a reef opposite the Glass Cove. It was impossible to save the vessel, and the crew were glad to escape with their lives. The wreck was a great attraction to local boys; once they stayed too long below and when they were hungry enough to come up on deck, the tide had come in and they couldn't get back to the beach. There was soon a rush of frightened mothers to the shore, who gave the boys a sound smacking before they got them home."

As a young boy in the early 1900s, George Currie helped out the emergency services in a small way. "We lived across the road from the police station, and on a Saturday night they picked up any drunk man who had gone to sleep on the pavement, put him in a grocer's barrow and wheeled him off to the cells. I used to earn a bit of money there because the constable would take sixpence out of the 'body's' trouser pocket and give it to me to take the barrow back to the shop! And the Fire Brigade used to get me and my pals to go up on a flat roof so they could practice rescuing us by making us slide down a canvas chute."

Fife girls who were in service in large houses or estates saw for themselves the difference in 'upstairs' living compared to their own home lives. "There was the servants' hall, the housekeeper's room and a room for any visiting ladies' maids," said Anne Penman, who was born in 1911 and worked for several titled or wealthy families over the years. "We were well looked after when the fruit was ready in the big greenhouses, peaches, white currants and raspberries. The lady of the house bottled her own fruit which took hours, and I washed all the Kilner jars in the linen room which itself was about the size of my whole house.

"You always had to knock on the kitchen door and a lot depended on what the cook was like. The kitchen had coal fired ovens for most of the cooking and baking, ovens where chickens were roasted and a spit fired by methylated spirits. I always found it politic to be friendly with the kitchen staff who gave us meringues and other fancy little things, we were all well fed. I was in fourth place between the housemaid and the parlourmaid; there was a lift which was pulled up and down on a rope between the kitchen and the dining room to transfer the food quickly. I also saw to the dogs' dinners, any leftovers were given to them. Everything was coal fired so there was a lot of dust, and no washing-machines, just scrubbing boards.

"The lady of the house in another family I was with in London was a partial invalid as she had been thrown from her horse when she was riding in Rotten Row. I helped her with her beautiful nightdresses, I had to stand on a stool to fasten all the tiny buttons. I had to dust her shelves of beautifully bound books with gold-edged paper, and then I took the ruler to make sure the books were perfectly straight. If they weren't, she would lie in bed saying 'The books on the second shelf need a bit of adjusting'".

In the years between horse-drawn transport and the motor car, tramcars where widely used. Kirkcaldy Town Council had its first trial run of the cars on 8 January 1903, and was tremendously proud of having the first tramway system in Fife (and one of the first in the UK). An early guidebook said 'Nothing that our Corporation has taken in hand has been done so effectively, so thoroughly satisfactorily or proved a source of pleasurable surprise to every member of our community as our tram cars.' The popularity of the trams is evident in the postcards of the day, when many street scenes in Kirkcaldy, Dysart, Dunfermline, Lochgelly and Coaltown of Wemyss often included a tram in the

The tram depot was in the Gallatown area of Kirkcaldy

6

foreground. Wemyss and District Tramway Company, founded by Randolph Wemyss in 1906, had distinctive single-decker trams popularly known as mustard boxes. They ran from East Wemyss to the Gallatown and were said to have carried millions of passengers over the 25 years they operated. Kirkcaldy's tram service ran until May 1931, finished off by deteriorating rolling stock and the advent of buses.

"I remember the last Kirkcaldy tram, there was no special ceremony or anything; once the cars were done away with, we used to play in the pits under the car shed in Oswald Road," said one man; while another said "The last time I saw one of the 'mustard boxes' was on the Leslie to Falkland Road where it was being used as a garden outhouse." And one Kirkcaldy man remembered his first sight of a motor car: "My parents took me through to Edinburgh on a holiday Monday and they said 'Look there you are, a horseless carriage', and it was making plenty of noise."

Motor charabancs came into their own for works outings where twenty or more passengers could be transported in relative comfort. The railway was also a popular choice particularly for holidays and days out before the Beeching cuts closed down many lines in Fife.

Every town and village had their own privately owned shops: some were so small that they were part of the owners' homes, particularly after WWI when so many women were left as widows. The front room with a makeshift counter served as the shop itself, or occasionally a garden hut was converted to take customers. Others were family businesses, with two or more generations of the same family working at the same time and often passing it down to the next.

The old Trades Directories show that even the smallest village had its own butcher, grocer and greengrocer, as well as specialist businesses such as coachbuilders, brush makers, saddlers, taxidermists and countless dressmakers, hat makers, shoe shops and drapers. Small shops had to get their stores from wholesale firms; one man remembered working in a wholesale grocer in Kirkcaldy High Street before items were pre-packed. "You had a scoop to shovel up oatmeal, barley and flour into bags," he said. "The carriers from outside Kirkcaldy flocked into the town twice a week and handed in their lines. Then they went off to have their piece, and came back to get the orders and laid them on to their carts. As an apprentice clerk I got five shillings a week, rising gradually by a shilling a week."

Grocers' shops were mainly privately owned, with the white-coated assistant behind the counter slicing bacon to order, cutting a slab of butter from a solid block and patting it into shape with two wooden bats, filling thick blue bags with sugar, or taking loose biscuits from glass-lidded tins for the customers. "Those of us who were children in the 1940s had a very plain diet compared with today. We had never seen things like avocados or peppers, and when bananas came back into the shops after the war, my pal thought you ate it with the skin on," said one woman. "All we knew of pasta was macaroni and cheese, and the only 'fast food' was from the local fish and chip shop. Very few people went abroad on holiday so we probably had the same kind of meals as our grandparents had."

With prices kept stable for many years under the Retail Price Maintenance Act, many women got their weekly grocery order delivered from their corner shop,

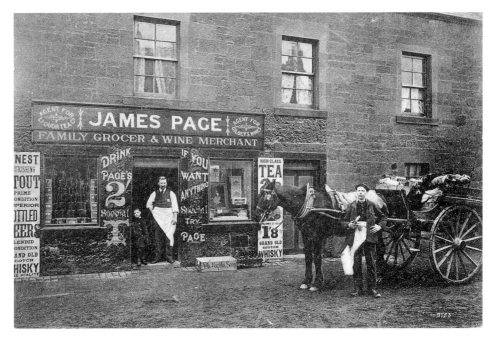

James Page of Cupar was typical of the privately owned shops of the day which sold a wide selection of grocery items.

Buckhaven Co-op was established in 1869 and its 17 departments catered for every need.

although sometimes customers abused the system. "One of our well-off ladies phoned the shop - not many people had the phone then - and asked for a tin of Brasso to be sent round to her house," said a woman who worked for a local grocer. "I thought that was ridiculous - she only stayed a couple of streets away - and I told the boss so. He said 'No no, she's a valued customer', and the message boy had to get on his bike and deliver it."

Most women however had a workable arrangement with their grocer. "You dropped your list into the shop and then in the afternoon the boy arrived at your door with your messages on his bike which had a carrier at the front for boxes," remembered a Fife grandmother. "Prices stayed the same for months if not years; you could send the children round with a list of staples like bread, milk and tea, and the money was the same every week." When RPM was abolished for most items, it opened the door to cut-prices and competition.

The Co-operative movement started in the 19th century, buying in bulk from local farmers who were given a guaranteed market, and re-selling at affordable prices to its members. For many families the Co-operative Society with its regular dividends was a lifeline, and everyone remembered their Co-op number. "The Store was a good thing because you got your dividend every six months, and it reassured a woman that she would have her rent earmarked." Buckhaven Co-op for instance advertised its advantages in 1925: "Members can be enrolled for one shilling for entrance fee and one shilling towards shares. Five per cent interest is paid on share capital, and each member is insured for life assurance with a penny in the pound deducted off the dividend to pay the premium. Our business includes grocery and provisions, bakery, drapery, boots, tailoring, millinery, boot repairing, joinery and funeral undertaking, and painting and paperhanging."

For those who were a distance from village shops, travelling carts and later vans came to them. "For years a fishwife came from Arbroath once a week with smokies," said a Thornton woman. "She was a great favourite, she came down by train and was dressed in her fishwife's clothes. A butcher came from Markinch with baskets filled with all the orders and my brother and I took them on to the farms. Johnny Mason's china cart came from Kirkcaldy, even the children loved it because it was built up with straw and the cups and saucers were stuck into the straw with the jugs hung round about it, it was lovely."

Milk was delivered daily. "Our milkman had a cart with two 10-gallon tanks with the brass spigots which let the milk run into your jug. No litres or pints, just guess work, a penny or tuppence worth. I had to go to the Co-op for messages with a wicker basket on my arm, I would run all the way and got a tram car back - I was glad to help my mother."

The major change in shopping habits came with the introduction of supermarkets in the 1960s. "When William Low went over to self-service we all thought this was wonderful: you picked out the apples or potatoes you wanted. There was the reflected glamour of what we had seen in American films, packing everything in tall brown paper bags - you didn't even need a shopping basket. We didn't realise then that this was the start of the decline and almost demise of wee shops and personal

Mrs Mavor's Millinery Warehouse in Dysart sold not only hats but a wide variety of clothes and underwear.

Tullis Stables was in Tolbooth Street, Kirkcaldy, and supplied horse-drawn cabs and hearses.

service in favour of giant supermarkets."

Menswear shops were common in every High Street. Hugo Melville, whose father founded the Kirkcaldy shop AK Melville in 1900, saw a lot of changes during sixty years in the trade and not in his opinion for the better. "I started just after the war and all the chaps were coming out of uniform, and a manufacturer in Leeds supplied us with cloth for suits provided we didn't sell them above £4 because they didn't want anyone to make a big profit. After that it was suits in February and March, and sports jackets and flannel 'bags' in April and May. Now you see jeans everywhere - we called them dungarees. Men wore headgear a lot - bowlers, Anthony Edens for the business and professional men, and flat caps for the chaps who worked in factories. Changed days."

Ladies had their own drapers' shops which were presided over by the owner. "I remember one quite high-class shop where the owner always wore a hat. Her stocks of blouses, sweaters and underwear were all kept in glass fronted drawers, and if you wanted something it was taken out and laid on the counter for you to examine. It took a brave woman to say that there was nothing there that caught her eye! Some of the favoured customers were allowed to take several dresses home to try on, and presumably to get their husbands' opinions on whether or not they were suitable. More down-to-earth shops had large cardboard boxes with 'winter vests', 'summer petticoats' or just 'knickers' written on the side. I remember when chain stores started putting dresses and coats on rails for people to look through without needing assistance, something which seemed revolutionary at the time."

The personal touch occasionally extended to banks. "My Aunt Bessie was with the Trustees Savings Bank, but she seemed to withdraw money more often than she put it in. One day the chief cashier shook his head and said reprovingly 'Wi' you, Bessie Chaplin, it's aye oot, oot, oot!' I can't see bank tellers today bothering about their clients' thriftiness or otherwise."

Before the National Health Service was established in 1948, health care was a luxury which many people could not afford and often went without, except in dire emergencies. "You had to pay the doctor to come for a home visit - it was half a crown, and you had to have the money on the table when he arrived. Our doctor came out to Thornton from Kirkcaldy, and he had a depot in one of the local houses where a lady kept all the pills. If you wanted the doctor - there were no phones except the public one - you had to get her to contact him and he would come up with his horse and carriage."

Dr Senga Greig recalled when her father set up his practice in their house in Townsend Place in Kirkcaldy. "He started as an assistant in 1910 and then took over the practice after a year. The surgery was in the house, the same as most doctors in the town, and one of the small rooms was still called the 'lab' when I was a child; as prior to chemists' shops, medicines were made up there and dispensed through the window! The previous doctor had a carriage with a white horse called Frenchie which the coachman would drive in one gate in front of the house and out the other. Our father cycled, and when he went to outlying farms he hired a pony and trap from George Tullis who had coaching stables in Tolbooth Street. There was a very good rapport between the doctors, and holidays and weekends were covered by mutual arrangement."

For those who found it difficult to afford a doctor's services, the Fife County Nursing Association provided an invaluable service where patients paid a small sum weekly and called on their community nurse at a clinic or asked for a home visit. The association's annual report in 1929 listed 50 branches throughout Fife with 63 nurses. The small sums from patients were not enough to fund the service, and local benefactors and fund-raising committees helped out. The report listed the refurbishment of nurses' cottages, fetes which paid for essential small cars, and gifts of clothing and money to help poorer families. Regular subscriptions of a penny a week were often collected through the collieries including Lochore, Cowdenbeath and Kelty. Those who could not afford a regular weekly payment or took the chance of not needing medical help could still use the service at a slightly higher charge.

One Fife woman remembered the era well. "We had a very well thought of midwife; she often didn't get paid for attending births because people just didn't have the money. Instead, people gave her sheets, table cloths and pillowcases from their cupboards as payment."

Not everyone chose conventional medicine: in Buckhaven, local herbalist David Taylor gathered his own plants and herbs and made lotions and draughts to cure common ailments. Known as 'Doctor Davey', he had a cottage near the Harbour Head and every Sunday there was a long line of cars outside his house as people queued up for his remedies. And a Dysart man recalled: "My grandfather had a chemist's shop and he kept leeches in a glass jar - folk who maybe had a bruised face after a row at the pub on a Friday night would borrow the leeches over the weekend and put them on the bruise. That cleared it up and they would return them to him on the Monday!"

# Chapter Two
# FIRST JOB

"I started at 14 as a helper to the miners; the shafts went three miles below the sea and we carried a gallon of water for drinking, which had to last two of us for the whole eight-hour shift underground. Sometimes we'd be hauling out the coal and working in water past our ankles; I was lucky, a few times I was just nearby when there was a cave-in or a flood."

For such a relatively small county, Fife in the early and mid-twentieth century was home to a wide range of industries including mining, linoleum, engineering, linen, pottery, paper making and newspaper production, as well as fishing and farming which were more ways of life than occupations. Every town and village had its own selection of small shops and businesses. The employment market has changed so radically since then that it seems like a different world. Computers and automation have taken over from many manual skills, forming a new kind of industrial revolution. Working conditions have improved for many, with health and safety measures, maternity and paternity leave, and childcare. There have been many steps forward: but with today's short-term contracts, sudden redundancies, long commutes and multi-tasking, perhaps there have also been some steps back.

Finding a job in those labour-intensive days was a far cry from today's interviews, presentations and politically correct adverts. Many jobs were heard about by word of mouth, often when another family member was already employed. This was not so much nepotism as a convenient arrangement for both sides; the employer knew the family and was satisfied with the standard of work shown, and the new young worker got on-the-job training often from an older brother or sister. Census records show that several members of the same family worked for the same business, often with different skills. Jobs then often were jobs for life, with workers being presented with their clocks (and occasionally a much more welcome easy chair) after fifty years of service in the same company.

Alexander Logan who was born in 1873 was one of the 'half-timers' who started work at Normand's linen mill in Dysart aged just ten years old. "I started work on the machines department and my wages were three shillings per fortnight. A few of us left there and started work in the rival mill for sixpence more, so we felt we were millionaires," he wrote in his memoirs. "You worked yourself up with your wages rising accordingly, finishing up in the reeling room at five bob a fortnight, feeling by then we were multi-millionaires." Even taking into account the huge difference in the purchasing value of the pound, his wages were surely below subsistence level.

"The conditions then were not much to write home about and some jobs were hard work. We started at six in the morning and finished at half-past past five, with two meal breaks between. A long day for a youngster but that didn't finish our day's work. To augment the household income, bags of hard 'tow' ropes were carried from the mill and along with parents and neighbours (the work was often pooled

Workers in linen factories had to stop talking once the machines started up as the noise was so loud.

Bakers in Westwater's Bakery in Dysart High Street.

Pupil teachers at Buckhaven School passed on their learning to fellow pupils.

and the money shared) we sat round in a circle teasing out the hard ropes to make 'tow', all for 3d per bag. They were hard days but great days: we were wage-earners, young people who mattered, and best of all we were helping our parents."

Many youngsters started their first job straight from school, with no knowledge of the work and no training beforehand. Ken Bowman from Pittenween started his working life at 14 delivering newspapers. "I began in 1925 and went round the whole town, the upper part first and then the shore, for six shillings a week. When I was sixteen I was apprenticed to the local baker, and the first thing that was needed was a white apron. Flour was imported from America in white sacks, so you were given half a dozen to take home to be made into aprons. My mother bleached them and made them up with tapes, so they covered you completely right over your day clothes; after that you had to buy your own sacks for sixpence.

"As an apprentice you worked on Saturday afternoons and then everything was tallied, and you got a box of cakes and cookies to take home. You collected your pay - it was nine shillings a week when I started which was good, people in other jobs only got five or six shillings so that was a fair amount and very welcome. One of the apprentice's jobs was to go to the butcher's every day and get maybe 6 lbs of mince for the pies and bridies. Although we didn't know about industrial dangers like inhaling flour, there were factory inspectors who went round all the bakeries. This didn't work as well as they thought - once they arrived at the first bakery, the apprentices would be send round to warn the others that the inspectors were coming."

In many jobs, green young apprentices were traditionally told to go to the nearest shop for a bottle of tartan ink, or a long stand. One young girl had her initiation on her first day at the flour mill being tossed into one of the large wooden troughs of flour, before starting her job of ladling it into 3 lb packets.

Teacher training was a mixture of hands-on experience and formal college study, and for one woman, training started when she was still a pupil at her secondary school in the 1930s. "I taught in the fourth year at Buckhaven, and got blackboard and talking skills long before I left school. I went from there to Moray House in Edinburgh for two years. Jobs were very scarce and there was a lot of poverty in the thirties, so you made sure you were well up on the training college list to help you get a job more quickly. Sometimes people didn't get a job for two years, with no dole money, but I was fortunate and got a job right away. I kept the piece of paper which told me to report to Thornton school, it was like a piece of gold, and my first pay was just over £2 a week. Then there was an economic crisis and teachers were asked by the EIS [the teachers' union] to offer back ten per cent of their pay; you just did it, it was helping someone else. There were 200 or so pupils at Thornton with nearly all lady teachers apart from the headmaster, so the classes were fairly big but it was the best size for both pupils and teachers. The desks were four in a row with benches and the children got their clothes blackened by sliding along them. I taught on Christmas Day because we got time off for potato holidays. I remember one old custom which had died out by the time I was a teacher; the second of April was 'tailey day' when you pinned dozens of paper tails on the teacher's back! He was a very strict teacher but on that day you were allowed to do that."

An efficient way to find new workers was to approach local schools for recommendations, when Ina Hutchison got her first job in one of the Kirkcaldy potteries. "They wanted an apprentice to learn how to paint and decorate the pottery, and they got me! They came to see our school paintings and they must have liked what I did because I got the job - I left school on Friday and started on the Monday." Another young girl had the same experience. "The headmaster was asked to recommend a pupil for the office at Morrison and Crawford's pottery. He wanted me to stay on at school but I was the second eldest of a big family and money was scarce. My mother said the only way she would let me stay on at school was if I didn't get a job - but for all the pay I got they could have managed without me. The doctor came round once a month to check the workers for lead poisoning from the paint; it was a very cursory look because if they had red-lead poisoning it showed round the top of their teeth. I had to run round and shout out 'Doctor!' and then get back to my work."

The ceramics industry in Fife (which included potteries in Kirkcaldy, Cupar and Inverkeithing) used a high proportion of young female labour, with much of the basic work being labour-intensive, repetitive and easily taught. Bella Barker started straight from school in a pottery handlers' department during WWI. "I made handles for cups and brown teapots and the two others I worked with made the spouts. You put the clay into a mould in the shape of a handle which was passed over to the men who stuck them on to the cups. You made up your mind to enjoy it because

A wide range of skills was needed in the pottery industry, including firing the kilns, making the pots and decorating them using different techniques.

there was nothing else you could do, but it was a very long day from six in the morning till six at night."

Kate Miller, another Kirkcaldy girl, started work at 14 to work at Methven's pottery in Links Street. "I got trained for a year and then you went on to piecework, you had to paint 36 before you got your pay. I was a hand-painter, you were told in the morning whether you were on plates, cups, saucers or bowls. You twirled the bowl round on a wheel as you painted the pattern with a bit of sponge or with a brush to do the leaves. It wasn't that easy keeping the wheel going and painting at the same time. Many a sore finger I had, we got that thick brown sticky paper to keep your finger from hurting but it still wore down. When you made a mistake in the design you threw it in the waste bin, sometimes I broke it so they wouldn't know who did it. We weren't supposed to talk when we were working but of course we did, I was always getting a row for that."

Young girls who were not employed in the pottery industry could still earn a few shillings by collecting pieces from the pottery bing and selling them. "We used to try and choose the best cups and saucers from the seconds," recalled one girl. "They would maybe be cracked or the design was wrong but people were glad to use them. My sister and her friend put pottery seconds in a clothes basket and sold them door to door."

And countless pieces of pottery shards - perhaps even some which Kate Miller broke - are still being washed up today, small reminders of a once huge pottery industry.

Going into domestic service was a popular option, a convenient arrangement for all concerned. Employers relied on help to keep their household running smoothly when labour-saving devices were minimal. Parents of young girls saw it as a good steady job where training in housekeeping would stand them in good stead when they had homes of their own.

Seconds could be collected from pottery dumps and sold round the doors.

Anne Penman, whose first job was in 1927 at the age of 16, felt she always had considerate employers. "My first job was working on a huge estate where they had cars, ponies and everything, and the lady of the house was very kind to her staff. You could move up to better positions as you learned more, so I started off as a housemaid and then a nursery girl to help with the babies; then parlourmaid where

Dorothy Sewing School Coaltown of Wemyss

The Wemyss School of Needlework, at the foot of Wemyss Castle drive, taught plain sewing, embroidery and smocking.

I cleaned the silver and laid the table, and then house parlourmaid so you got a lot of experience. The family had a big square pew at the front of the church and the staff sat behind them every Sunday, a lot of work tailed off on Sundays. I wore a dark grey dress with a white apron and a cap to keep your hair tidy. It was all black stockings and if you got a hole in them you used a black-lead brush to cover it up. I think we got ten shillings a week but that included half a crown to send our nice white aprons to the laundry."

A similar 'them and us' situation was found in the School of Needlework in Coaltown of Wemyss, which started in the 1870s when Dora Wemyss (later Lady Henry Grosvenor) found the wife of an estate worker wandering about in a state of depression after the loss of her child. Miss Wemyss engaged her to do plain sewing in Wemyss Castle, and then sent her to the Royal School of Needlework in Kensington for training. She then started up a sewing school in a room at the castle which soon relocated to a building at the end of the drive on Coaltown's main street. The school took in village girls at 14 as apprentices to be trained in needlework, embroidery and smocking for orders from aristocratic families.

"It was quite an honour to get into the school," said former worker Mrs Adamson. "I was there for eight enjoyable years, you were sewing for the gentry and some of the highest in the land. Your parents put down a deposit of ten shillings when you were taken on as an apprentice, and after six months you got that back and got a wage. You really worked on anything to begin with and you didn't get your money back if you weren't suitable. You made samples of all the different stitches to show you could do them, it was strict discipline but the training was excellent."

One of her contemporaries, Mrs Lambert who was born in 1905, had the same experience. "I had my name down for six months and started when I was 14 - it was an honour to be accepted, but no-one said very much about the wages! I got five shillings a week for the first year, paid monthly so you had to wait for it, and as you were trained there you were expected to stay on."

A young onlooker whose father worked on the Wemyss estate used to watch the girls going to work. "I can still see them walking down the road arm in arm, either singing or walking smartly - almost like a line of chorus girls and smartly dressed. They had to take great care of their hands in case they got caught on the silk and fine lawn. I think it must have been a hard apprenticeship - as children we were never allowed in the building but we watched the ladies going in with their beautiful dresses and big hats."

Family connections were often useful in finding a job. "My brother David was with the *Fife Free Press* and told me they were needing an apprentice," said Bob Ritchie who was born in 1901. "I have a note yet from Mr Strachan [of proprietors Strachan and Livingstone] which set out my wages: 4/3d a week and then a shilling rise for the first five years. Setting the type was all done by hand, so the apprentice would get to do maybe a church notice, copying the one from last week. The [First World] war was going on and when someone joined up, I was put on to working as an operator, setting type for a whole day at a time. I stayed with the *Press* for 54 years until I retired."

Collieries throughout Fife were a major source of employment, and Wullie Colville started work at the Lady Blanche pit in Dysart in 1920 at the age of 14. "I could have worked at three pits in 24 hours. If you didn't like it at the Blanche, you could have come home at half-time and started at the Lady Victoria in West Wemyss or the night shift at the Randolph. When I worked at the Lady Blanche, I went down at 5 am and walked underground about two miles to the Dubbie [the Frances pit] to collect three pit ponies and take them back to the Blanche. For that I got the handsome sum of 6d and had to take them back down again in the afternoon. We had seven days off at the Fair in July and two days off at New Year, all unpaid, and no Christmas holidays," he said. Another Dysart man had much the same experience when he went to work in the mines in 1925. "It was a hard life, the young laddies went with an older man and you had to carry the explosives and the man's drills," said Tom Carrington. "A lot of young boys went with their fathers, but my father was Pilot at Dysart and Leith so you just went with anybody. You had to walk downhill under the water, the coal seams were 24 ft thick, and fill at least 17 tubs of coal a day to make a wage."

Even in the mid-1950s the employment situation was very different than today. "When I finished at secretarial college you could pick and choose from the job adverts and decided which one would suit you best, there were columns of adverts for shorthand-typists," said one Fife woman. "My dad was an accountant and said 'You could get a job in a commercial firm and get a better pay, or you could go

Fife had several collieries where the work underground was hard and often dangerous.

Kirkcaldy Cottage Hospital was gifted by Michael Barker Nairn in 1890, with a circular extension added later.

into an accountant's office with less money but meet more boys!' That was an easy choice for me and I was the only girl among eight fellows - I think I went out with each of them in turn. My dad was right about the money, I got £4 a week in 1956 which wasn't much even then.

"I don't know that the firm was actually dodgy but I think the boss must have been sailing a bit close to the wind. When I noticed that some of the postage stamps were George VI and not our present Queen, he said not to use them on any letters as they might have to be used to back-date agreements! When he was called to an Inland Revenue tribunal because he was behind with his clients' tax returns, he sent me along instead. I was in the waiting room with all these professional men, and I still remember the secretary looking at me and saying with a sigh 'I think we'd better see you first.' They realised what I hadn't, that the boss had only sent me there to give him more time to get in the returns. It was fun to work there though, when the boss was away on an audit I took in my knitting if I was on my own, or a table tennis set so we could play across the desks. I can't imagine having the time or opportunity to do that today."

In some cases, particularly fishing or farming, sons followed in their fathers' footsteps, and it was common for a fisherman's daughter to marry within the fishing community. "My father worked with the horses on a farm, and we had a free house with a garden and free potatoes, forbye the wages," said Mary Dobson. "I left school at 12 to go on the farm, the first job I got was hoeing beans and then on to potatoes and turnips. We helped with the hay and the harvest and got an extra shilling a week for that."

A Lochore woman started her training as a nurse in the late 1930s in Kirkcaldy Cottage Hospital, before going on to Edinburgh City Hospital. "We did four years including a year of fever treatment. There were different grades of uniforms - first a white short-sleeved dress and cap, then as you progressed you got on to navy blue and by the fourth year you were in deep blue. Local doctors came in to see their patients and sometimes you would go with them; if you didn't have your cuffs on you had to rush and put them on. You were called by your surname by the senior staff though the patients just called you Nurse.

"I did my training in theatre which not everyone had the chance to do; some of the instruments were so old the chrome was coming off. I remember once I was carrying the X-ray plates for the professor and another four men - the plates were dripping wet and I slipped and went down just like that, but still holding the X-rays. The men just walked on, they probably thought the nurses were always falling at their feet! When I qualified in midwifery I worked in Glasgow for a time; we had a lot of work in tenements and the conditions were dreadful, the families were desperately poor. Oh dear, when you came home you just dropped everything in the bath and washed yourself from top to bottom."

One Fife woman remembered her mother talking about her first job in a wholesale pharmacy in the 1920s. "One of the girls was carrying a large jar of hydrochloric acid when the stopper came off and splashed the acid down her dress. The material dissolved and most of the front of her dress just disappeared. One of

The *Mars* was a former battleship from the Crimean War and was adapted to a training ship for boys needing supervision or protection.

The young boys on the *Mars* wore naval uniforms and were trained in different trades. They are pictured here on a summer holiday in Elie.

the young male clerks took off his jacket and wrapped it round her to protect her modesty. My mum would say 'Of course men were gentlemen in those days!' The other story she told was much worse, one of the men was lifting down a big glass jar of strychnine when it fell on the floor and smashed. He got a shard of glass in his finger and automatically sucked it, and he dropped dead there and then. I know we sometimes think that today's Health and Safety rules go a bit too far, but in those days there were none at all by the sounds of it."

One rigorous and surely unique way of training for future employment was given on board the *Mars* training ship for boys who were seen to be at risk. Although it was perceived to be a centre for young offenders, many of the boys were orphaned or vulnerable and might fall into crime if left in their home surroundings. The *Mars*, a former battleship which had served in the Crimean War, was converted to a training ship for 400 boys and a dozen instructors. The young boys were kitted out in small versions of naval uniforms, issued with a hammock and bedding, and underwent strict discipline. They were trained in various trades such as woodwork, tailoring, gardening and shoe repairing, and in the evenings there was football or boxing, or practising in the ship's bands or choir. They gave gymnastic exhibitions and concerts on shore which helped raise funds for the ship, as did the sale of their vegetables and woodwork. The local boys were allowed occasional visits home, and sometimes helped landowners during the shooting season. Each summer they had a holiday in a disused granary on Elie pier where they played football and swam as well as giving musical entertainment for which they were rewarded with cakes and lemonade.

The *Mars* provided good training for boys who might otherwise have ended up unemployable or even in prison; they left the ship with a variety of skilled trades or equipped to join the Navy. But with the benefit of hindsight, we can only speculate at the personal cost which that training involved.

Linen workers from Normand's linen mill in Dysart paraded to the station for their annual trip in the early 1900s.

Workers in the Links Pottery in Kirkcaldy left for their annual outing around 1920 in a local charabanc owned by the General Motor Carrying Company.

# Chapter Three
# LEISURE TIME

"We spent hours helping my Uncle Arch to polish the brasses on the harness for the horses the night before the factory trip. We scrubbed the coal cart and spread clean straw on it and then decorated it with coloured paper chains."

In the early to middle years of the twentieth century hours of work were long - Saturday working was the norm - and days off were few and far between. Leisure time was particularly precious and was put to the best possible use. It wasn't until 1938 that an Act of Parliament pointed the way by establishing permissive (but not compulsory) holidays with pay. By the end of WWII 80% of workers had gained paid holidays, usually one week in the year, largely through union negotiations.

In the meantime, many of the larger workplaces organised day-trips for their employees using hired horse-drawn brakes which were later replaced by motor charabancs. The works' outings were special occasions when employers and employees mingled at least for that one day, with sightseeing, meals and often impromptu singing and dancing as the day progressed. The season for outings started in June, leaving at six in the morning and returning home at 10 at night, with a full page of reports published each week in the local papers. Each place of employment had its own excursion, with everyone from tramway men to newspaper staff going to Perth, Aberdeen, Montrose or Pitlochry with electricity workers even taking the train to London for the weekend.

Dysart man Alexander Logan remembered the annual Normand's linen mill trip in the early 1900s. "What a great day that was, on a fine summer Saturday morning the workers would gather at the factory gate. It was a great sight to see the hundreds of happy smiling faces, with both women and men decked out in their best clothes. The sun shone on the bright uniforms of the bandsmen and on the large banners carried by the tenters and mechanics. The bands would strike up and then the huge throng would march to the station en route for Perth or whatever town they chose that year. Then the home-coming at night with songs and fiddle and accordion music, that was a night I'll always recall."

St Andrews Merchants' Association had their annual trip on the local holiday in June, using railway, bus or steamer transport. Rothesay and Loch Lomond were popular venues as were Aberdeen and Braemar.

Working on the railway had its own perks, as a Thornton woman explained. "Half of Thornton worked for the railway - the other half were miners - and they got a day's holiday without losing a day's pay which was a big benefit. When I was wee, the family had two free passes for the trains. A whole faction of Thornton went on what was called the No. 5 Tour, which was very popular; you went up Loch Lomond and across Loch Long, into the Clyde and then to Craigendoran and then home by train. It took a whole day with the trains all connecting with each other, so Thornton children were all very knowledgeable about Loch Lomond!"

One man decided to make his own arrangements for a seasonal celebration. "I started at the pit in 1920 when we got seven days off at the Fair, no holiday at Christmas and two days off at New Year, all without getting paid," said Wullie Colville. "I saved up a shilling a week and then I had a glorious burst-up on New Year's Day. I got the train to Edinburgh for half a crown, then up the Mound to the museum and the Castle - both were free - then down to Holyrood Palace. Back to Leith Walk for a pie and chips and then to the gods in the Theatre Royal for the pantomime. After that, a real splash out for a three-course tea with grilled herring or smokie to start off, then bacon, sausage, egg and chips, with a pot of tea, toast and cake all for half a crown. I finished up with a walk to the Empire, the Lyceum or the Kings and then the train home from Waverley with still enough left to buy a fish supper."

The coastal villages still have their maritime galas: St Monans with the Sea Queen, Leven has the Rose Queen, Pittenweem has the Fisher Lad and Lass, and since 2009 the Scottish Fisheries Museum has revived the Fisher Lass and Lad as a joint celebration for Cellardyke and Anstruther. "It was usually the crews of the boats who ran it, if they had a good looking daughter they would put her in for it. The boats used to go out and then come into the harbour in one long line with the lassie on the first boat, and she would come ashore and walk through the town."

Yawl racing, using open wooden boats around 17ft long with a lug sail and a 26 ft mast for racing, was another event held every summer. Bags of sand and the weight of the four-man crew were the only ballast in races which were tests of skill and seamanship. There was always particularly fierce rivalry between crews from West and East Wemyss and Dysart, with supporters going round the regattas to follow their favourite yawl. The afternoon's racing was followed by celebrations or commiserations at the local pubs, and one (possibly apocryphal) story was often told about one Dysart crew who had a resounding victory at the West Wemyss regatta and celebrated well into the night. Finding their way back to the harbour in the dark, the crew rowed strongly for home but after two hours were no nearer their home port. When dawn broke they discovered that no-one had got round to loosening the mooring rope and they were still tied to the pier.

Fife's rural communities paused in their daily hard graft to meet their friends at the annual agricultural shows. One of the most prestigious was when the Royal Highland Show - which travelled to different locations before its permanent home in Ingliston - was held near Cupar in 1912. Ploughing matches were keenly contested in various local venues, with prizes given for everything from highest standard of work and best turnout to straightest furrow, oldest ploughman and ploughman with the largest number of children.

Music has always played a big part in Fife culture, with brass or silver bands playing for both entertainment and  competition. The annual Raith Band Contest was held in the grounds of Kirkcaldy's Raith House on the third Saturday in August. In its heyday it attracted around 30,000 people to hear and see a fiercely competitive display. Although Kirkcaldy Trades Band was naturally a strong favourite, the contest brought bands from other parts of Scotland such as Brechin,

Raith Band Concert and Flower Show was held each August in the grounds of Raith House.

Forfar, Lanark and Falkirk as well as the north of England. The competition was organised by Kirkcaldy Horticultural Society which held its flower show, also hotly contested, on the same day.

Many of Fife's coastal towns and villages had regular visits from troupes of pierrots who entertained their audiences from open-air platforms near the beach. "The pierrots had a special stage with seats for visitors and railings round it; they charged for the seats but we children stood outside the fence and watched it for free," said a Leven woman. "Big names at the time like Flanagan and Allen toured before they hit the big time, I saw them at Buckhaven. There were lovely sands there before the coal bing at the Wellesley Pit got washed into the sea and ruined them."

In St Andrews, pierrots such as Bliss's Busy Bees performed on the beach pavilion near the Step Rock outdoor swimming pool. They gave two shows a day in the 1930s until their public grew dissatisfied with sitting outside and preferred the summer variety shows in the Town Hall. The summer entertainments were not always trouble-free; in Burntisland rival sets of pierrots caused a disturbance until the Council gave the bookings to Fred Collins of Glasgow for the season.

Dance halls were tremendously popular in Fife as elsewhere, and many young people met their future life-partners on the dance floor. One of the more modest dancing schools was Currie's in Kirkcaldy which taught new steps to the young dancers - popularly known as Currie's Jumpers - and held a Saturday night dance. "My father started the dancing academy in the early 1900s when he built our house in St Brycedale Road with the dance hall at the back," recalled George Currie who was born in 1898. "He held group lessons for learners on weekday evenings with classes for individuals on Tuesday nights. The ladies sat down one side of the hall and the gents on the other, so my father would take a girl up on the floor until she got the hang of the steps like the Charleston or the Black Bottom. Then he would take hold of one of the boys and just fling them together so she could teach him. When I came back from the war I helped in the evenings to demonstrate the new dances, but I couldn't have made my living from it. I worked at Barry's [linoleum factory] through the day and then took over when my dad retired. The band had their own day jobs and got something like five bob each for playing all evening."

Saturday nights were the highlight of the week. "I still get stopped by people saying what great times we had. I tell them 'Aye, it was your first venture in life' because some of them came when they were still at school. Their parents wouldn't have let them go to the big Palais in the Arcade or any of the other big ballrooms, but we were a small friendly place. We never had any bother - maybe because we were across the road from the Police Station. There was no bar, all they had was lemonade from a crate from Douglas's round the corner. The one time they brought in bottles was on Old Year's Night; we took the bottles off them until they left to go first-footing and there was never any trouble."

Burntisland had the grandly titled Palais de Dance in Manse Lane, which advertised itself as 'the most popular palais with the perfect floor; where youth and pleasure meet, to chase the glowing hours with flying feet.' Wednesday was the popular night and Saturday was the carnival night, with special dances during the holiday season. It attracted an older clientele, so those who wanted a livelier evening went elsewhere. "We liked the Kinema in Dunfermline because the band played new tunes, it filled up quickly so you had to make sure you got there early. There was a dance teacher so you could copy her if there was a new dance."

Not many employees got the chance to attend grander affairs. "I worked as a housemaid in a big house near Stirling, and I was a member of the Young Conservative Club and there was a big dance coming up," said Annie Napier. "I bought my dress, it was hyacinth blue satin scalloped at the bottom and a ruffle on the shoulder. The family were in London so the housekeeper said we would have to ask the lady of the house first in case she wouldn't let me go. The factor called for me in his van to take me to the dance but no letter giving permission had arrived, so I never got to the dance. Next day the letter came from London saying 'I do hope you let little Annie go to the dance'," she said, the disappointment and the memory of that unworn dress still cutting sharp even after eighty years.

"A circus used to come to Thornton in my father's time, one tent had a notice saying 'See the horse with its head where its tail should be.' Everyone was queuing up but when you got in, it was just a horse standing the other way in its stall," said one woman. "My father always told of the time when he was a wee boy when they were watching the elephant, and it put its trunk out and pulled hold of my grandfather. The circus man said 'It's not hurting you, it must know you.' My grandfather kept looking at the elephant and speaking to it, then he lifted up its foot and there was his regiment's name stamped on its foot. So the elephant had recognised him from all these years ago - no wonder they say that elephants never forget."

Ceres Games, the oldest in Scotland, date back to 1314.

Annual Highland Games included Ceres, Markinch, Newburgh, Burntisland, St Andrews, Thornton and Inverkeithing. "Thornton Highland Gathering came off successfully with an attendance of 50,000, with a squadron of 90 police on the ground drawn from all over the county," reported the *Fife Free Press* of July 1911. A Thornton woman recalled: "My father in law used to keep count, once he got up to 63,000. A lot of people cycled to the Games and people put up notices outside their houses saying 'cycles kept here' so they could leave their bikes safely. There was a big dance at night and folk came from all over; you had to watch who you had the last dance with because you had to take her home, so it was a blue do if your partner came from Leslie or Kirkcaldy!"

The Co-operative movement held galas in their local area with races, Highland dancing and brass or pipe bands. "We each got three shiny new pennies; the well-to-do bairns had enamel mugs but us poor ones had 'tinnies' or tin mugs round our necks and a poke of biscuits and cakes. The Miners Gala in June was a red letter day, we packed into a train for Edinburgh or Perth and then back home for a singsong in the square."

Local hospitals before the NHS relied heavily on donations from the public, and Kirkcaldy Hospital Pageant was an annual summer event when businesses and individuals competed to produce decorated floats and costumes. Local linoleum firm Barry, Ostlere and Shepherd for instance not only decorated their lorry as an advert for their products but the girls on the float wore dresses entirely made of linoleum.

"The judging took place in Gallatown Park," said a *Fife Free Press* report in 1930, "and then the mile-long procession headed by two mounted policemen and

One of the floats in Kirkcaldy's Hospital Pageant in 1924 with linoleum manufacturer Barry, Ostlere and Shepherd's entry.

The Jolly Boys provided impromptu entertainment in their summer camp.

accompanied by pipe bands went through the town to Beveridge Park. The streets were lined by thousands of people and the traffic was stopped. Pathhead and Sinclairtown Co-op had a lorry representing a shepherd and his sheep, Nairn's had a Puffin' Billy drawing a large shoe with Mother Hubbard and her children, Dysart Co-op had a model battleship and the Girls' Club were Greek dancers." Even after the NHS came into force, the pageant continued to draw huge crowds and raise large sums for charities. "The Lang Toun and Lass were elected each year, it was a great honour to be chosen, and they had a limousine in the procession," said one local woman. "All the decorated floats and individuals had collecting tins out, some put them on long poles so they could reach the folk looking out their top floor windows, the community spirit was amazing. It finished up at the Girls' Club on the Prom when the Lad and Lass presented prizes to the winners, and then they went on to the Cottage Hospital with flowers for the patients."

Alfresco camping was popular especially when money was tight, and the *Fife Free Press* in July 1911 reported: "There are over 200 young men residing in private tents on the shore at Kinghorn between Pettycur and the Alexander III monument, a record number. The young men are mainly from Glasgow, Airdrie and Edinburgh and have called their camps The Jolly Boys, The Naughty Boys or the Woodbines."

Street entertainment was varied and often drew large crowds. "We saw the dancing bear with a German band in lederhosen and braided tunics with spiked helmets - it was just before WWI and we thought they were great until the rumour went round that they were German spies."

Brass or silver bands have always been well represented. "The players had to stand and play in a square with the conductor in the centre," said Harry Briggs from the Dysart Band. "There were no proper music stands, just long boards to hold their music and we carried these for the outdoor Sunday evening concerts. It changed its name to the Dysart Colliery Band around 1912 and miners paid a penny a week towards the costs. There were a lot of bands - Dundonald, Wellesley, Coaltown of Wemyss and Bowhill (that was a great band) - with a lot of rivalry. We would go to the Miners' Gala in Holyrood Park for the band contest and joined up with the miners with their banners."

Quoits or kites was a popular game of skill and strength particularly among the mining communities. As there was illegal betting on the outcome, the game often took place in quiet spots like the Wemyss woods or even the caves at East Wemyss. "The miners used to come to Dysart to play and we used Sailors Walk as a grandstand. Wally Walters of Lochgelly could toss a 14lb quoit from 21 yards right on to the pin. You could lay a gold watch on top of the pin and it would never be harmed - of course I never used my own watch!"

Royal coronations or jubilees were celebrated with great enthusiasm. George V's Silver Jubilee in May 1935 was marked in virtually every town and village with processions, fireworks and bonfires. St Andrews Boys Brigade took a congratulatory message from John O' Groats to London. Bonfires were lit on top of every hill including Largo Law, Falkland Hill, Benarty and Clentrie. There were fancy dress balls in Leven and Strathmiglo, sports for children and adults, concerts in

Quoits was a popular game of skill with heavy - and illegal - betting on the winners.

Auchtermuchty and Ladybank, and a march-past of school children in Kirkcaldy watched by 15,000 people. Many towns gave each child a Jubilee shilling, with the jovial comment from Leslie's Provost Paterson: "This shilling will be your very own to do what you like with!"

There seemed to have been only one slightly sour note. A newspaper report headed "Communists' opposition gathering" said: "There was little in the way of celebrations in Cowdenbeath. At the Central Workshops, Mrs Reid the wife of the general manager planted two commemoration trees. In the evening a silver birch was planted on behalf of the Young Britons of the town." So that local children did not lose out, a treat for 200 youngsters was held but - to underline the point - not until the next day.

# Chapter Four
# WORKING LIVES

"All the women were kept busy baiting lines through the day, what a speed they worked at. They baited outside in the winter because there was a smell from the mussels. It was a hard life, no doubt about that, I can't think you would get women to do that now."

Working conditions in virtually every job were hard with long hours and often low wages. Training was usually done on the job with help from a more experienced worker, and the work itself was often very specific and specialised.

The fishing industry was one of Fife's mainstays with the herring boom in the late 19th and early 20th century making it an important way of life. Many of North East Fife's coastal villages had their own fishing fleets including St Andrews, Crail, Buckhaven, St Monans, Anstruther, Largo and Pittenweem.

"Our house had a garret at the top of the house to keep the fishing gear, there were six of us and each person had a part of the garret for their nets, pallets and taws which were the stoppers which joined the nets," said a Pittenweem man who had fishermen on both sides of his family. "The first council houses built in Pittenweem after WWI all had garrets; that was Abbey Park and before then it was called Salmon Park because that's where the salmon fishermen kept their gear. The winter herring fishing made quite a lot of money but that ended with the war. Sometimes they went to Whitby or South Shields using big lines for herring and then they would go to Peterhead from June to August, the summer drave. They went to Yarmouth from October to December, if it was bad weather they could be away for weeks and never caught much. They were reasonably well off but after WWI things just collapsed, no German markets which about finished the herring industry. It didn't start to pick up until the late twenties and thirties when they had new and smaller boats. During WWII they all started using the seine net and used it ever since, it took up everything which ruined the fishing industry.

'I don't think they were allowed to use seine nets in the Forth except in small boats but they trawled for prawns and scallops quite successfully. Some of them went to France and got some good hauls. You could trawl down and get nothing and then go back over the same ground where the prawns came back out of the mud and get good catches."

The 1916 Fife Trades Directory reflected how important the fishing industry and its suppliers were to the local economy. Anstruther and Cellardyke had five waterproof and fishing material manufacturers; Johnstone Brothers were listed as rope, twine and sail makers, St Monans had Easson, Nicol and Robertson who supplied oilskins, and Pittenweem had two marine stores.

There was also a flourishing net factory, Cardy Works in Lower Largo, which employed around forty people. They made heavy-duty nets for the fishing industry, and the strips of guarding at the edges of the nets were put on by hand by workers

Fishing was an important part of east coast life; this image of Largo pier shows the day's catch being landed.

Women in the fishermen's district near St Andrews harbour cleaned mussels which were used to bait the lines.

Distinctive Fife fishing boats included the Fifie, the Baldie and the Zulu.

in their own homes. Owner David Gillies must have been a thoughtful employer for the times as he allowed his workers to play bowls in their lunch break on the green laid out in front of the factory.

East coast fishermen used mussels for bait, kept alive in scawps - rough enclosures above low-water mark - until they were taken out at low tide (although local laddies sometimes helped themselves for their own fishing). The fishing lines were checked regularly to replace any missing hooks which were baited with around 800 shelled mussels. "Shelling mussels wasn't so bad in the summer when you could do it outside, but it was a heartbreak in winter. The knife went into the mussel which scooted out into the dish, by that time you were soaking and you had to keep washing the floor to get rid of the smell; and there were always cats around to see what they could pick up."

The Fifie was one of the best-known herring fishing boats with vertical stem and sterns; it was followed by the Baldie (named after the Italian Garibaldi) and then the Zulu, but the sailing boats eventually gave way to the steam drifters in the early 1900s. A notable survivor is the *Reaper*, a 70-ft Fifie first registered in Fraserburgh in 1901 and bought by the Scottish Fisheries Museum in Anstruther in 1979 where she was restored to her original condition. The *Reaper* is berthed at Anstruther and sails down the coast manned by volunteer crews for gala days and educational visits as well as starring in television documentaries.

The fishing industry declined sharply when the shoals of herring moved away. Perhaps the worst casualty was Buckhaven harbour when its surrounding rocks became covered with colliery waste leaving no protection against the tides. "The most imminent peril of the harbour is that it is being silted up with redd, and a black barrier five feet high lies right across the entrance," reported the *Fifeshire Advertiser* in 1929. "Only after the tide has been half flood can small boats pass out or in. Six motor boats are fishing from Buckhaven beside the yawls but the harbour is accessible to them for barely two hours at high water. Any boat striking the bank would be in danger of being swung broadside on and capsizing against the steep slope." The first breach in the harbour wall came after a great storm in June 1936, and Buckhaven Town Council's debate was reported in the local paper. "When the Provost said that the storm had done it, a councillor replied 'No, the storm finished it but the damage was done by underground workings. Now the rocks are all covered, it is like a beach that gave no shelter and the wall got the full force of the waves.'" Once the harbour wall was breached, the whole fabric of the pier was exposed to the waves; and over the course of a weekend in January 1937 thirty or forty yards of the east pier were swept away with the elements disposing of the rest.

"There was a lot fishing in Dysart before WWII, first haddies and then flounders, lobster and partans too," remembered Tom Carrington who was born in 1911. "The Dysart men put their boats in the water every first of June, they had a crane but they mostly just threw the boats over the edge of the pier. Some of the men made a good living out of it, the lobsters went to Edinburgh and the rest they took round the doors with a hand barrow. There was a lot of rivalry, one of the Anstruther fishermen said to me that our haddies were getting to the right size and they would be down to

Joan Clark from St Andrews was dressed in the typical fishwife's costume.

Minto Colliery in Lochgelly was one of many pits operational throughout Fife.

clear them out. Right enough, three weeks later their boats came down and took the lot."

One of the best known fishwives in St Andrews at the start of the 20th century was Joan (pronounced Jo-Ann) Clark who wore the traditional costume of a striped skirt, tight bodice, red shawl and a fisher apron. The local fishermen supplied her with white fish and flounders, and she had a fish shop in Market Street as well as wheeling her barrow delivering fish direct to housewives. In common with most fisherwomen, she had very high standards of housekeeping and her house was always immaculate. Thought to have been the last fishwife in St Andrews, she died in 1927. And a Fife man recalled: "There were always two Newhaven fishwives with blue and white skirts and blue flannel blouses in Edinburgh's High Street selling saucers of whelks and mussels, food for the gods."

Mining was one of the biggest industries in Fife, a hard and often dangerous job with long hours spent deep underground. "I remember when the pit-head baths were opened in 1951, a real milestone and we were like a lot of playful puppies larking around. We never had so much water to wash in, before that every drop had to be heated on the fire," said miner Wullie Colville. "I once had to take a ship's captain and crew to the coal face, he was about 20 stone, the fattest man I had ever seen. We helped him into a wooden coal hutch and I had to push it all the way, when we arrived back at the pit bottom he rewarded me with the princely sum of a silver threepenny bit. Another time we had a captain and crew who walked all the way, and when we came to the surface the first mate said 'Boy, I'll climb the highest mast you can find, but I'll never go underground again, that's just for rats and rabbits.'"

There was very little machinery in many trades in the 1920s with most of the work being done manually. Baker Ken Bowman explained: "We used to set the hand-made dough from flour, water, yeast and salt and that was laid to rest in a wooden keg and left overnight. You made that into bread the next morning, and added any fat or sugar you wanted and put it to lie for a couple of hours. The plain bread was made in pairs stuck together, so a half loaf was 2 lbs. The apprentice had to stamp each one with 2 lbs right in the centre when it came out of the oven, it had to be that weight as otherwise you broke the law.

"We had to take our weights to get checked once a year, everyone was very particular. During the war you had to take what was going, the flour was sort of brown and sometimes you had to substitute soya flour. There wasn't much in the bakery I didn't do apart from running the batch, that was when eight dozen plain loaves were baked in a special domed oven - it was a specialised job which the foreman did by himself. It took maybe two hours to bring the coke-fired oven to the right heat. We never bothered about flour inhaling, we didn't know about industrial dangers then though folk claim damages for that now. We had to work it out so as not to have waste, if there was too much bread left the folk would wait for the price to go down. There were no women in the bakery itself when I started, though later on they did things like icing and decorating which was an artistic job if you spent time on it."

The bakery department of Dysart Co-op made wedding and christening cakes as well as bread and everyday essentials.

An example of the beautiful sewing carried out in the Wemyss School of Needlework.

Work in linen factories required skill, stamina and dexterity.

Linen manufacture played a large part in the Fife economy with hand loom weaving in virtually every village before power looms took over. Kirkcaldy is thought to be the first in Fife to operate power looms in 1821 followed by Dunfermline and Leslie. Auchtermuchty, Cupar, Dysart, East Wemyss, Falkland, Freuchie, Ladybank and Strathmiglo all had thriving linen factories. The industry initially concentrated on plain domestic cloths for sheets and towels and then developed to include more unusual or luxury items. Normand's works in Dysart made linen for covered wagons in pioneer America, while Dunfermline mills made fine linen and damask for Holyrood Palace and exhibited their samples at the British Industries Fair in 1938.

'There were about eight linen factories in Kirkcaldy when I was 15," said Margaret Ness who was born in 1913. "I was a weaver with Blyth's and while most of the factories did sheets, we were famous for 'ticking tikes', dark blue and white covers for mattresses or bolsters. The process before me was done by the drawers who drew the yarn into looms and then it went to the dressers who dressed it with a kind of starch so the yarn would stand the strain. We were all happy in our work, you were allowed to speak to each other until the power went on when you wouldn't be able to hear above the noise."

Hand sewing was a speciality in the Wemyss School of Needlework in Coaltown of Wemyss. "Miss Russell who was in charge sat at a high desk in the showroom and took orders from the ladies who came in, we didn't see them at all," said Mrs Lambert who started there at 14. "You had to go in and show her your work to see if it was up to her expectations which were very high. Fire screens had to be soaked in water and stretched out on the floor, and one morning a girl came in and walked right over it. What a state Miss Russell was in, we had to show her the soles of our shoes to find out who it was, but mind you it was an awful thing to happen.

"There was a treadle sewing machine for making the long side seams on nightdresses but apart from that it was all hand sewing which the ladies expected. Smocking was quite difficult, you drew it up on a piece of wood with pins on it. Lady Victoria [Wemyss] had eight smocked dresses done for one of the baby boys, white with blue smocking, and we all did a pram cover with blue daisies. Meg Simpson was the tracer who pricked out the pattern and marked it with ink which went on to the cloth beneath. When we got an order from Canada for children's dresses, Mrs Russell cried me ben to try them on as they fitted me because I was so wee."

One of her fellow workers, Mrs Adamson, said: "We wore aprons and white sleeves from wrist to elbow with scissors attached by a tape to your apron. You had to look after your hands in the winter and use skin lotion so the silk threads wouldn't catch on them. Everyone thought that the girls who worked at the school were special, you were in among the gentry all the time and it was very interesting - you were sewing for the highest in the land and you met quite a few of them."

Another kind of fashion was also well catered for. "My Aunt Nan was a milliner and went to London in the early 1900s to one of the big hat makers for experience," said a Leven woman. "She came back here with her sister and started up business for the ladies who all wore big hats at that time. She did all her mum's hats too, she would make a frame of very thin covered wire and covered it with georgette or other materials, all hand done including a lining. She had two milliners working for her and in the front shop there was a glass case with all the little ribbons, posies of flowers and feather which she used to decorate her hats."

With public transport a priority, Effie Ewing from Buckhaven worked as a bus conductor when she was 16. "We wore white coats or navy blue ones in winter with a number on them and you looked up the drivers' rota to see who you were on with. I was at Aberhill depot, they started you off with local runs and then you finished up with long distance runs to Perth or Newport. You had a wee square of wood for the tickets with a punch and your cash box before we got a modern machine where you set the prices on a dial and just turned a handle. We had blackouts on the windows during WWII and the bus lights were shaded. There was a wee flap in the blind at the front so you could see where you were in the dark and you had a torch for the road-end. The miners didn't have pit-head baths then and came on in their working clothes, so the bus company sent buses with seats which we could wipe for the miners' regular runs. My dad was a miner and when I was wee I ran down to meet the 'Whippet' - the miners' train. We children used to fight to see who got the bit of his left-over piece, it always tasted better having been down the pit!"

Picture postcards were a favourite way of communication especially when a message could be posted in the morning and delivered the same day. Local booksellers and printers sold a wide selection of views of towns and seaside resorts. Davidson's in Kirkcaldy High Street both printed and sold postcards, and Mrs Allan whose uncle latterly owned the business worked in the shop. "They had their own photographer to take the views and they were made into sets of Kirkcaldy or Leven which they manufactured under the name Ideal Series. They specialised in the Heather Calendar with Scottish views with a spray of real heather from a farm near Ladybank; they broke it up into little sprays and pressed them and glued them on the front, they were very popular to send abroad."

The pottery industry was a large source of employment. Kirkcaldy (which had four major potteries including Fife Pottery which made the highly collectable Wemyss Ware), Cupar and Inverkeithing all produced the huge quantities which were essential before the days of plastic. It was a specialised industry involving different trades including handlers, throwers, kilnmen, transfer makers, crate maker and decorators. "There was a painting shop but we never went in there as we felt they were a step above us," said one woman whose daily job was to stick the handles on cups and teapots.

Anne Penman's jobs in service introduced her to a variety of people. "One of my posts was in South Kensington where the head of the family was Comptroller to George VI; he was always very polite and always lifted his hat to me when he met me outside. I was allowed to go along to Buckingham Palace to watch the procession so I could catch a glimpse of him. Out came the Queen (later the Queen Mother), she had lovely dark blue eyes and a smile which seemed to be just for me. I was very impressed to see my employer sitting beside the King in the car, more so than to see the King I think!

"Another family had a villa in the south of France, I went as a housemaid and

Anne Penman (left) outside her London employer's house.

did a lot of fetch and carrying for the lady's maid. Not many people in Fife had the chance to go to Cannes in those days so I knew I was very lucky. Her butler was very smooth and charming but I didn't like him at all. There was a spate of robberies of jewellery and silver in the Riviera and it turned out he was one of the gang, madam had to go and identify him. Next time she heard from him was on a letter headed HM Prison."

On the other side of the labour divide were the employers, the owners of the factories and coal mines. Although seen as being light years away from the daily grind of their employees, theirs was a different kind of responsibility. "My father came to Dysart in 1919 to start a carpet business, starting out with an old fashioned loom which originally was for linen," said Janet Meikle. "He was always ahead of things and went on to spool Axminster with mass production and then took over another factory and built a new weaving shed. We later branched out into patterns and colours, and then went into the export trade where you had to get more colours to suit each country's tastes. He always insisted on the best materials despite the cost as he wanted quality.

"I was one of the employees initially and kept the same hours, working through all the different departments - design, spooling, winding and weaving. When my father died, I became managing director in the days when having women in charge of firms was still a rarity. My sisters and I ran the business together, and my grandfather who helped out as general tradesman and was a favourite with the workers as he listened to anyone who had problems."

Medical families often continued in their fathers' footsteps, and Dr Senga Greig joined her father's medical practice in Kirkcaldy in 1947. "I started originally for six months hoping to go off for further experience before I came back, but due to father's failing health I stayed until I retired in 1982. As in most practices before the Health Service, the staff consisted of the doctor's wife or mother who answered the phoned, tracked down the doctor in emergencies, gave advice, and comforted

Allen Litho printers are pictured designing and printing sample books of linoleum patterns.

patients and their crying babies who could be safely left in their prams at the front door. My mother often coped with minor injuries and along with my sister and myself sent out the accounts."

Local newspaper played a big part in keeping people up to date, reporting both national and local news. "*The Fifeshire Advertiser* was the first paper in Kirkcaldy, it was in circulation years before the *Fife Free Press*," said Bob Ritchie who worked on the local papers from the 1920s. "The *Press* came out on a Saturday with eight pages but you could only print four pages at a time which you did on the Friday afternoon. Then at 5 am on the Saturday you reversed the sheet and printed on the other side. I started as a compositor and then progressed to being a linotype operator, which was a great thing at the time as it was a keyboard machine. A compositor had to stand setting up one letter at a time producing a column of type which could take a whole day, whereas a keyboard operator produced a whole line in a couple of minutes and did four or five columns. When it was finished you just melted it down instead of having to put all the type back in the box.

"During the war we had to publish photographs of the men who were killed in the war, very very sad. Photographs were difficult to get because nobody made the blocks locally but we got them sent on from Edinburgh by train and put them in the *Press* the next day. We had a midweek paper *Kirkcaldy Times* so we started at 3.30 am to get it in the shops for teatime. It was an 8 am start on Fridays for the *Fife Free Press* and you worked on without even a cup of tea until your dinner hour, and you just kept going until we got the paper finished. Finishing time was supposed to be 5.30 the next morning but I remember walking home one Saturday morning at 8 am when the girls were coming down to start their work in the shops. We distributed the paper to the newsagents by tramcar and paid a penny for each bundle of papers and maybe give one to the tram driver. The original proprietors Mr Strachan and Mr Livingstone were still there in my time although they were well on in years."

And another Kirkcaldy man had his own light-hearted memory of the local paper. "My brother worked with the *Press* and then went on to the *Glasgow Herald*. He and his pal printed off £5 notes on the presses but they were so daft they didn't realise they should have put a different serial number on each of them!"

# Chapter Five
# ENTERTAINMENT

The Lammas Market in St Andrews still draws large crowds every August.

"Ladies and gentlemen, I am now going to show you the latest novelty secured at vast expense. It is called Living Pictures or Kinema, and the scenes which I will now show on this expensive machine are the very latest."

The typically flamboyant language of the travelling showmen was used to advertise the bioscope, an early form of silent movies before the 1920s when virtually very town and village had its own cinema. The bioscope first appeared at Kirkcaldy Links Market in 1904 with often as many as five or six shows put on by different operators. The *Fife Free Press* of 1909 gave a glowing account of the new attraction. "The shows are of the cinematograph order in a style of magnificence quite new to the district. The outside stages are much superior to the old-fashioned exhibitions, illuminated with electric light and equipped with excellent fairground organs."

Westerns, contemporary murder trials, patriotic features, slapstick and Scottish favourites such as Harry Lauder all featured on film; in addition, early documentaries were made with people leaving their works or factories. "My grandfather Billy Codona used to travel with the shows in the summer and do the cinematograph in the winter," said show-woman Minnie Paris. "He advertised

'Come to the fair and see yourself on film,' and always got good audiences."

The tented bioscope had an outside stage where young ladies dressed in frills and picture hats danced to attract customers, and the films were silent with someone playing the piano in the tent. One local man recalled his early memories in the *Fifeshire Advertiser*.

"I saw a notice saying 'Great New Novelty: Living Pictures, admission one penny', so I paid my money and entered a small booth with a white screen at the back. There were no seats, and in the middle were a couple of empty boxes on top of which stood a machine which was then called a magic lantern. The proprietor turned the handle while a strip of thin glazed paper fell to ground; I was close to him and about to light a cigarette when he told me not to throw the match on the paper as it might set it on fire!

"The show ran for four minutes with two film with no titles, sound or captions. The first showed a lady and gentleman, presumably newly married, and she was removing some of her clothes. After a minute and a half she still had three times as much on as you would see on any pretty girl on a Sunday afternoon, but then it was daring for a woman to display her ankles. The other showed a soldier and a nursemaid with a child in her arms in a railway carriage. He was anxious to kiss her as they came to a tunnel, but when they came back into the light he was found kissing a part of the bairn's anatomy instead of the pretty nursemaid." Daring stuff - and surely good value for a penny.

Travelling fairs were - and in some cases still are - looked forward to with anticipation. Kirkcaldy Links Market, the longest street fair in Europe, can trace its origin back seven hundred years. Show families such as Wilmot, Cadona, Pinder, Horne, Paris and White have been travelling to the Market like their fathers and grandfathers before them. "We lived in the Sands Road before the Prom was built up and I could lie in bed and watch the Market being set up," recalled John Crichton who was born in 1900. "All the showmen's gear and living wagons were drawn by horses, and children's roundabouts were driven by turning a handle. Then steam engines were introduced which had to be topped up all the time with men wheeling water barrels from the roadside taps. No electric light, just paraffin burners which hung underneath the stalls. They had side stalls with anything you could throw a wooden ball at, including seconds from the nearby clay pipe factory. When push bikes came in and were still novelties, they had bikes on a circular track spaced out quite close so they could get as many as possible on at once, and you paid to pedal round.

"Later on when I became a postman I had an awful job to deliver letters to the stall holders. Eventually you got to know their names and where they stood, and if there was a bunch of them standing talking you could just hand their mail over to them all."

Nancy Brodie whose house overlooked the Prom loved the arrival of the Market. "White's Waltzer was right opposite us, and we could see old Granny White going round to collect the drawings from the ride until she was in her nineties. We could watch the showmen putting up the prices on Friday and Saturday nights, or reduce

AGRICULTURAL SHOW, CUPAR.

The Agricultural Show in Cupar around 1900 drew large crowds of visitors and traders.

them when business was slow. The roundabouts were just built on old lemonade crates, of course that wouldn't happen now."

Pink sugar hearts were made by confectioner 'Paurley' Kidd who took a stall at the Market every year. "He passed on his recipe to my parents during the Depression when they were struggling for money," said Kidd's great-grandson. "Some were white and some were pink, and they had a secret ingredient to make them fluff up."

A lesser known and much smaller fair in Kirkcaldy was the Pathhead Market in Mid Streeet and Back Street in July, which closed in the early 1900s. St Andrews has its Lammas Market in August with shows and side stalls, many operated by the same showmen who attend the Links Market. Cupar had St James Fair, originally a feeing market for farmers to find seasonal workers but latterly solely for entertainment.

The late 1920s, right up until the advent of television, was the golden age of the cinema. Picture house owners competed to have the most exotic names: the Electric Cinema in Cowdenbeath, the Alhambra and Hippodrome in Dunfermline, Cinema de Luxe in Lochgelly and the Opera House in Kirkcaldy. Where there was no actual cinema, Anstruther and Elie used their town halls, and East Wemyss had a small picture house which attracted people from the other Wemyss villages who walked along the shore. Filmgoers knew not only the names of every contemporary movie star but also their off-screen activities in Picturegoer - so little has changed with today's celebrities, real or transient. Queues formed for 'early doors' at each new film, with children allowed in by bartering empty jam jars - not always washed first - for admission.

There were always new gimmicks: the manager of Dunfermline's Palace Kinema

The Port Brae cinema in Kirkcaldy, designed by local architect William Williamson, was one of the many picture houses in the town at that time.

The Corn Exchange in Kirkcaldy hosted many interested and varied acts.

was dinner-suited James Rich who advertised 'Always a rich programme of pictures shown.' The Musketeers' Theatre in Cupar had their own cigarette packets with their name between blue theatre curtains, produced by local tobacconists Courts and Son. When the silent film Dawn (with Sybil Thorndyke playing Nurse Edith Cavell) came to the Normand Hall in Dysart in 1928, there were five showings a day with a special bus which could be hired from all over Fife.

The Palace in Methil's High Street advertised two shows each evening, and the local guidebook of 1947 said: "Generous provision has been made for indoor entertainment. Methil has the Palace and the Imperial, the Globe is in College Street in Buckhaven and Denbeath has the Western Cinema." There were weekly silent pictures in Anstruther Easter Town Hall in 1912 (3d for adults, 2d for children). The Empire opened in the town's Cunzie Street in 1919 in a former brewery building, and the first night's proceeds of £12 were donated to the Nursing Association. Anstruther had the Regal which was opened in 1934 by Provost Carstairs and was said to have taken 100,000 bricks and ten weeks to build. With two projectors and special sound system from London, its first film was Footlight Parade with James Cagney.

"I remember seeing the Palace, the Port Brae and the Rialto being built," said a Kirkcaldy man. "The Rialto's first film was The White Sister starring Lillian Gish, a real tear-jerker." The local paper of the day gave a full description of the Port Brae cinema's opening night in November 1913. "The new Kirkcaldy picture house at Port Brae was opened by Hon. Sheriff Substitute RC Lockhart in the presence of a large invited company. An interesting programme was shown with dramatic and amusing films along with beautiful travel scenes. The pictures were projected with fine clearness on a screen with intensified light. The building, planned by Mr William Williamson FRIBA was greatly admired by the guests. Tip-up seats are provided and the sloping arrangement of the floors permitted an uninterrupted view from every point." An improvement surely on another local cinema: "You went up to the 'gods' and climbed up and up the stairs. There weren't seats, it was just a stone platform with no back."

Before the 'Talkies' were introduced, the script ran along the foot of the screen to explain the action. "When I was wee I went with my mum, and you could hear all these women's voices reading it out loud," said one man. Another had the same memory: "One woman used to read the titles out to her pal so you made sure you didn't sit beside her because you could read it faster than she could. There was always a cliffhanger at the end in the days of Mary Pickford and Pearl White, so you had to go back next week to see what happened. When you were older you went to the Saturday second house, you'd really made it by then."

Bob Ritchie remember the cinema in the Corn Exchange in Kirkcaldy's Cowan Street. "It was known as the BB, short for the Bright and Beautiful Cinema. They also had performances from travelling companies who added to the cast by calling up members of the audience on stage." Another local man recalled "I remember Dolly Robson singing a requiem for the *Titanic*; the last two lines were 'And the band was bravely playing the song of the Cross and the Crown; Nearer my God to Thee, as the

The Adam Smith Hall and Beveridge Library were opened in 1899 by Dunfermline-born Andrew Carnegie.

The audience in the early days of the Byre Theatre in St Andrews were so close to the stage they could have almost touched the actors.

ship went down.' There wasn't a dry eye in the house and she received a standing ovation."

Dunfermline's Opera House in Reform Street was built in 1903, a two-balconied, lavishly decorated building seating 1250. It was never home to opera but concentrated on plays, farces and musical comedies. Top stars in the 1930s such as Harry Lauder and comedian Will Fyffe (who wrote the iconic I Belong to Glasgow) appeared there. It closed down in 1955 and was demolished to make way for a new shopping mall in the 1980s. That wasn't the end of the Opera House story: most of the interior fittings including its ornate plasterwork, box fronts and some of its plush seating were carefully dismantled and shipped to Sarasota in Florida, where it was reborn as Asolo Repertory Theatre.

The King's Theatre in Kirkcaldy, later the ABC, was a magical place for Wullie Colville. "My grandmother took me there when I was five, and the sight of the painted cherubs and angels on the ceiling never left me. When the orchestra started tuning up, the lights were dimmed and the safety curtain was pulled up in a magical hush. Joseph O'Mara was a grand tenor singer and held the last note of an aria across the stage, no microphones then, just natural sound. They were all C companies - London had the A company and Edinburgh and Glasgow got the B, but we delighted in every minute. There were artists like Harry Gordon, Dave Willis, the Houston Sisters, and Sammy Thomson whose catch phrase was 'Tak' the ship up a close, Captain, Ah'm awfy seek.'

"We all gathered in the street for the last night of Kirkcaldy Amateur Opera's annual production to watch the grand folk in their finery and the doorman with a megaphone summoning their carriages. George Tullis in Tolbooth Street had some fine carriages to hire, but most of the gentry had their own - Captain Michael and Lady Victoria Wemyss, Sir Michael and Lady Nairn, and Captain Oswald of Dunnikier all attended."

The origins of the Byre Theatre in St Andrews have a unique place in theatrical history. Founded in 1933 through the inspiration of local journalist and playwright A.B. Paterson, it was transformed by a group of enthusiasts from a disused cowshed into a small theatre. It was initially run by the St Andrews Play Club, who supplied cushions for the audience before second-hand seating was acquired from a local cinema. Part of the charm was that the auditorium was so small that the front row of the audience were almost sitting on the stage. With the advent of road-widening and new house building, the theatre was demolished and a new Byre was built a few yards from the original. It was rebuilt and extended in 2001 and attracted both professional and amateur companies.

The Normand Hall in Dysart was the venue for many variety events. "One woman came to do a turn, she went under the name 'Can U Lift Her?'" remembered Tom Carrington. "All the big Dysart men who fancied they were strong would come up on the stage when she said 'I'm only seven stone', that's all she was. Then it was like she started to put on weight, eight stone, nine stone, and got so heavy they couldn't lift her off the floor, I never knew how she did it. Dr Bodie did tricks and mesmerised people - when electricity was just coming in, he got folk to hold a

St James Market was held in Cupar every August. Originally a hiring fair for agricultural workers, it was latterly a travelling funfair.

cable and then put the current on. I suppose it would be very mild but they got an awful fright and started screaming!"

Many big names came to Fife when they were starting out on their careers, including Elton John, David Bowie and Pete Waterman. But the night which will never be forgotten was when the Beatles came to the Carlton Cinema in Kirkcaldy in October 1963.

"My pal and I got tickets because his mother worked with the Carlton Bakery which did the catering for the acts in the show," said Dysart man Jim Swan. "They had two performances with 1500 in the audience for both shows. Our seats were five rows from the front, and what I remember most was the noise from the audience, you couldn't actually hear the Beatles singing at all. Because we had heard that Ringo loved jelly babies, folk in the gallery threw jelly babies at the stage - not single ones or packets, but whole boxes which landed on us. My pal's mum got them to sign our programmes and I treasured that for years along with my ticket stub and a playbill. I kept them in a brown envelope until we moved house about ten years ago and they somehow got lost in the flitting. I'd rather not think of what they would be worth now!"

Kirkcaldy's Carlton cinema with its art deco frontage opened in 1930.

The programme - for those who heard it - included From Me to You, Please Please Me, and Twist and Shout. The Beatles played two houses and at the end of the second show the crowds were so dense that four of the Carlton bingo stewards put their coats over their heads and rushed out of the side fire exit as decoys. The Beatles themselves ran out of the front door into their open-topped Austin Princess and were whisked away to Perth.